THE UNOFFICIAL GUIDE TO TEAMWORK IN MINECRAFT®

JILL KEPPELER

PowerKiDS press

Published in 2026 by The Rosen Publishing Group, Inc.
2544 Clinton Street, Buffalo, NY 14224

Copyright © 2026 by The Rosen Publishing Group, Inc.

All rights reserved. No part of this book may be reproduced in any form without permission in writing from the publisher, except by a reviewer.

First Edition

Editor: Greg Roza
Book Design: Rachel Rising
Illustrator: Matías Lapegüe

Photo Credits: Cover, pp. 1, 3–24 SkillUp/Shutterstock.com; Cover, p. 1 Soloma/Shutterstock.com; Cover, pp. 1, 3, 4, 7, 9, 10, 12, 14, 16, 19, 22, 23, 24 gersamina donnichi/Shutterstock.com; Cover, pp. 1, 3, 4, 7, 9, 10, 12, 14, 16, 19, 22, 23, 24 Oksana Kalashnykova/Shutterstock.com; p. 5 Pressmaster/Shutterstock.com.

Cataloging-in-Publication Data

Names: Keppeler, Jill
Title: The unofficial guide to teamwork in Minecraft / Jill Keppeler.
Description: Buffalo, New York : PowerKids Press, 2026. | Series: The unofficial guide to Minecraft social skills | Includes glossary and index.
Identifiers: ISBN 9781499452990 (pbk.) | ISBN 9781499453003 (library bound) | ISBN 9781499453010 (ebook)
Subjects: LCSH: Teamwork (Sports)–Juvenile literature. | Teams in the workplace–Juvenile literature. | Cooperativeness in children–Juvenile literature. | Minecraft (Game)–Juvenile literature.
Classification: LCC HD66.K47 2026 | DDC 302.3'5–dc23

Manufactured in the United States of America

Minecraft is a trademark of Mojang (a game development studio owned by Microsoft Technology Corporation), and its use in this book does not imply a recommendation or endorsement of this title by Mojang or Microsoft.

Some of the images in this book illustrate individuals who are models. The depictions do not imply actual situations or events.

CPSIA Compliance Information: Batch #CSPK26. For Further Information contact Rosen Publishing at 1-800-237-9932.

Find us on

CONTENTS

WE'RE A TEAM 4

WHAT IS TEAMWORK? 6

TEAM COMMUNICATION 8

SHARING SKILLS 10

GOOD LEADERS 12

SUPPORT SYSTEMS 14

HONESTY IS BEST 16

INDEPENDENCE WITHIN A TEAM . . 18

BE PROUD! 20

GLOSSARY 22

FOR MORE INFORMATION 23

INDEX 24

WE'RE A TEAM

When you start a new *Minecraft* world, you'll usually have a goal. Sometimes, this goal is nothing more or less than just having fun! Maybe you have a further goal such as building something really cool or exploring as far as you can. And maybe, if you're in a shared world, you want to work together and have fun with your friends.

But things can get far more **complicated** when you add other people. Even good friends can have different opinions and ideas on how to do things. You and your friends will have to figure out how to work as a team if you want to **achieve** your biggest goals.

MINECRAFT MANIA

Different **versions** of *Minecraft* have different world sizes. *Minecraft* worlds are generally huge! They can extend for millions of blocks in all directions.

If you and your friends want to play together, you might play on a *Minecraft* server. This is a computer in a network that provides services or files to others.

WHAT IS TEAMWORK?

You've probably been on teams at least a few times. Maybe you play a sport like baseball or soccer. Your gym class at school might divide players into teams. There also might be reading teams in your classroom or something similar.

Cooperation and teamwork are close to the same thing, but not quite. Cooperation is working together toward the same end and helping others do so as well. It's part of teamwork, which is the effort of a team to achieve a common goal. In *Minecraft*, this could be mapping out a huge section of your world, building an amazing base, or **defeating** the Ender dragon.

MINECRAFT MANIA

 Maps in *Minecraft* show the **biomes** you've traveled through in different colors and patterns. You can put a map in a frame in your base to show the area! Make a frame with eight sticks and a piece of leather.

People have built some amazing things in *Minecraft*, including huge modern houses, great stone castles, and even entire cities.

TEAM COMMUNICATION

Communication is very important to teamwork. It's important to know who on the team is doing what so people work toward different parts of the goal. And, of course, it's important to **define** what the goal is in the first place!

For example, in *Minecraft*, a team of players might decide they want to build a central base, then send out explorers to map the surrounding area as far as possible. They'd have to communicate to reach this goal and to figure out what they need in a base and how to build it. Then they'll need to figure out who's doing the mapping and in what direction.

MINECRAFT MANIA

 You can "zoom out" a *Minecraft* map to show more space. A starter map shows about 128 blocks by 128 blocks, but it can be zoomed out to show 2,048 blocks by 2,048 blocks.

You need a cartography table or an anvil (and more paper) to zoom out a *Minecraft* map. The more times you do it, the more area the map will show.

SHARING SKILLS

One part of good teamwork is recognizing that everyone has different skills and making use of those skills in the best way possible. Maybe one friend on the team doesn't like exploring so much but really likes to build things in *Minecraft*. Another enjoys exploring and is good at *Minecraft* wilderness survival.

It wouldn't make much sense to make the explorer build the base while sending the builder out to map things! A good team works together to use their skills in the best way possible. People also tend to work more effectively on things they like to do.

MINECRAFT MANIA

Minecraft has dozens of kinds of blocks that you can build with. This includes multiple kinds of stone, including plain gray stone, cobblestone, granite, diorite, andesite, deepslate, tuff, sandstone, and versions of each!

GOOD LEADERS

A good team usually has a good leader, someone who steps up, makes plans, listens to people, and **assigns** jobs. This can work in different ways. Some groups will pick their leaders based on what they can do. Sometimes, people become leaders without even meaning to, just because they do what needs to be done.

A good leader in our *Minecraft* example would recognize who should be doing what jobs. They might also keep track of what the base needs and supplies for the explorers. Leaders make everyone feel included and support people in doing their jobs.

MINECRAFT MANIA

Our *Minecraft* mapmakers in these examples might need a lot of paper. You can make one sheet of paper with three pieces of sugarcane, which grows near water.

SUPPORT SYSTEMS

One of the good things about a good team is that no one works alone. This doesn't mean that someone will be hanging over your shoulder at every moment! Some people like to work on their jobs by themselves. But it does mean that if you need help or **feedback**, there's always someone there to ask.

Imagine our *Minecraft* builder needs an **anvil** for the base. However, an anvil takes a lot of iron, and iron is used for many things, so they don't have enough supplies. In a team, they could ask one of their teammates to do some mining while they continue working on the base.

MINECRAFT MANIA

To make a *Minecraft* anvil, you need three iron blocks and four iron ingots. To make a block of iron, you need nine ingots, so that's 31 ingots altogether!

To make iron ingots, you need iron **ore**. Then you need to smelt, or heat, it in a furnace to make iron nuggets. Nine iron nuggets make one iron ingot.

HONESTY IS BEST

Part of communication in a team is being honest with each other. Sometimes teammates will have to say things like, "Hey, maybe it would work better if you did it this way," or "You're not doing enough to help, and it's causing a problem. How can we make this better?"

In a good team, the people saying this will be kind and have **empathy** for the person who's struggling. And that person will listen and be honest with their teammates and with themselves. Maybe they need some help, or a different job (like mining instead of mapmaking) would be a better fit.

MINECRAFT MANIA

Mining is an important job. After all, it's right in the name of *Minecraft!* Mining is how you find ores, which give you the materials to further build and explore the world.

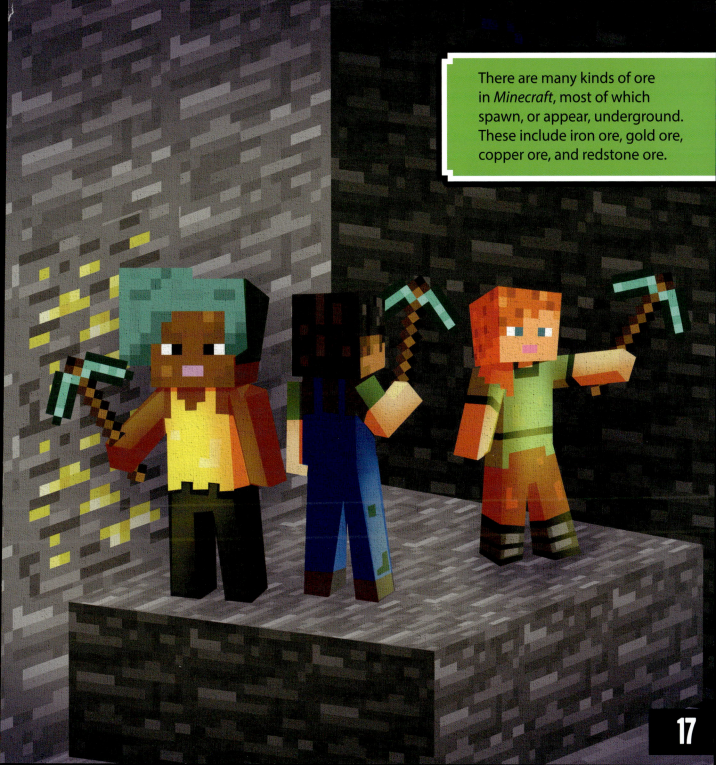

There are many kinds of ore in *Minecraft*, most of which spawn, or appear, underground. These include iron ore, gold ore, copper ore, and redstone ore.

INDEPENDENCE WITHIN A TEAM

Even though it's good to have support in a team, it's also important to have some independence. Good teammates don't have to have someone watching them all the time to do what they're expected to do. Teammates need to trust each other to get their jobs done so everyone can succeed.

For example, if a good *Minecraft* fighter goes out exploring with a *Minecraft* mapmaker, they need to pay attention to protecting their teammate, not just wandering around while they work. What would happen if a creeper sneaks up on the mapmaker while the fighter is picking flowers? Nothing good!

MINECRAFT MANIA

 Creepers are sneaky. Unlike other *Minecraft* monsters, they don't make a sound until they're right next to you and ready to blow up!

It might be good to use the buddy system when going out exploring. One buddy can watch the other's back!

BE PROUD!

It's always great to achieve a goal. Imagine how you'll feel if your team works together to make a big goal happen! It's good to have a sense of pride and accomplishment for something you worked hard for, whether it's an amazing *Minecraft* base with a giant map wall or a good grade on a group project at school.

Working with a team is something you'll probably have to do a lot in life. It takes skills like honesty, leadership, and communication. It teaches you how to better support others and recognize and value your own skills. Teamwork will always be important.

Imagine how big a map you can create in *Minecraft* if you work together!

GLOSSARY

achieve: To get by effort.

anvil: A heavy iron block on which metal is shaped. In *Minecraft*, an item used to repair things, rename items, and combine enchantments.

assign: To give someone a task or amount of work to do.

biome: A natural community of plants and animals, such as a forest or desert.

communication: The use of words, sounds, signs, or behaviors to convey ideas, thoughts, and feelings.

complicated: Hard to explain or understand, having many parts.

defeat: To win a victory over.

define: To determine the qualities or meaning of something; to show or explain something completely.

empathy: Understanding or being aware of and feeling the emotions of others.

feedback: Helpful information that someone gives to show what can be improved.

ore: A source from which valuable matter is obtained.

version: A form of something that is different from others.

FOR MORE INFORMATION

BOOKS

Mojang AB. *Minecraft: Epic Bases*. New York, NY: Del Rey, 2021.

Munsch, Robert. *Teamwork*. Toronto, Canada: North Winds Press, 2021.

Olsen, Shannon. *Collaboration Station*. Life Between Summers, 2024.

WEBSITES

Map

minecraft.wiki/w/Map

Learn more about maps and mapmaking in *Minecraft*.

What Can You Mine in Minecraft?

wonderopolis.org/wonder/What-Can-You-Mine-with-Minecraft

Wonderopolis provides background information on *Minecraft* and what you can do in the game.

Publisher's note to educators and parents: Our editors have carefully reviewed these websites to ensure that they are suitable for students. Many websites change frequently, however, and we cannot guarantee that a site's future contents will continue to meet our high standards of quality and educational value. Be advised that students should be closely supervised whenever they access the internet.

INDEX

A

anvil, 9, 14

B

buddy system, 19

C

communication, 8, 16, 20

cooperation, 6

creeper, 18, 19

F

friends, 4, 5, 10

G

goal, 4, 6, 8, 20

H

honesty, 16, 20

J

jobs, 12, 13, 14, 16, 18

L

leader, 12, 20

S

skills, 10, 20